DOWN ON THE CORNER

DOWN ON THE CORNER

Poems by Kevin FitzPatrick

MIDWEST VILLAGES AND VOICES · MINNEAPOLIS

Some of these poems have appeared in the following magazines and anthologies: *The Alley, Attention Please, Barque, Blossoms and Blizzards* (Pegasus Prose), *Buckle, Event, Gathering Post, Hungry Poet's Cookbook* (Applezaba Press), *Kudzu, Lactuca, Lake Street Review, Light Year '86* (Bits Press), *Loonfeather, Milkweed Chronicle, New Poets Anthology* (Cherryable Brothers), *North Country Anvil, Poets' Voices 1984* (San Diego Poets' Press), *The Poet, Sackbut Review, Sanctuary Si!, The Selby-Lake Bus* (Lake Street Review Press), *Sing Heavenly Muse!, Thirteen, Tower Talk, Twin Cities, Visions* (Black Buzzard Press), *Wyoming: The Hub of the Wheel—A Journey for Universal Spokesmen*, and *X: A Journal of the Arts*.

Midwest Villages and Voices
3220 Tenth Avenue South
Minneapolis, Minnesota 55407

Library of Congress Catalog Card Number: 86-90561
ISBN 0-935697-02-0
First edition
Designed by J.B. Sisson
Cover photograph by Tina Marie Blomer
Manufactured in the United States of America

For Corinne and Bernard

CONTENTS

ONE

IRENE'S CAFE

Irene this morning
washes dishes first
then glances at customers
like leftover beers

her tattooed cook
wearing a ski jacket
scrambles eggs
while pouring coffee
in our empty cups

along her horseshoe counter
we are all silent
churchgoers at the Consecration
waiting
for the first drunk to enter
to offer her marriage

so Irene will laugh
so the jukebox will play
so Sunday will begin

GREAT CUBE ICE COMPANY

"Understand that until a machine is made,
we're a-gonna have to do it."

We understand when he shuts the power off,
defrosting the darkened warehouse starts:

long two-by-fours as poles, our palms cupping
the ends, must poke frost from the far ceiling

fast before pallets of bagged cubes drip
penny-a-drop through the cracked wood floor,

and we understand cold hunks
of this white ceiling collapsing through dark

must thud against our bodies
as we dodge slowly, balancing the tottering poles,

and we understand, sort of, his
"we're a-gonna have to do it" means

he will be away in light at his desk
doodling up machine after bizarre machine.

WHERE WORK IS SCARCE

It is not safe to be out of work around here
where work is scarce.
Your apartment will be held together by one nail,
and when anything goes wrong, if the sink plugs up
or the radiator drips,
your landlord will find out and begin hammering the nail,
its blue shaft will speed across your kitchen floor,
your apartment will become smaller each minute you're not
   at work.

It is not safe to be out of work around here.
As you search for work, the streets will be slick with
   railroad tracks,
signal men hidden in smoke will caution your crossing,
mechanically waving blackened lanterns
as gray trains pass no louder than breathing,
or trucks will bully you down blocks of deserted streets,
dark wet warehouse streets that never drain,
that blur in and out of parking lots,
streets that finally narrow between steep factory walls
but still wide for trucks to scrape through as you stumble.

It is not safe to be out of work around here.
Your father, who lives in a time when there was plenty of
   work
and who will be steps away with news of a temporary job,
will be crazy from days of searching for you:
a tip at the loading docks that you're just down the street,
a tip down the street that you're over playing pool,
and he will be crazy from the humming of metal,
the humming of metal that never stops around here,
that will skim away fine curls of flesh from his brain
like a carpenter's plane with a razor edge,
until finally he will bend curiously over your body,
then continue on a tip toward the stockyards.

13

BLOOD PLASMA CENTER

"Earn $100 a month!
Help hemophiliacs part-time.
Ideal for students, housewives, and clubs.
Become a professional donor now."

If any club has answered this ad,
it's the drinkers who meet all day
behind Addison's Bar on Franklin.
They're here like me because they're broke.

Aisles of donors in easy chairs,
their arms attached to plastic tubes
draining into pouches of blood.
The music over the sound system
is the disco version of "Let It Be."

As a nurse sticks my needle in,
I concentrate on *Bobby Sherman Always*
tattooed forever on her wrist,
then stare at the man across from me
as my blood spurts through the clear tube.

He is getting settled in his chair,
leaning back like someone's dad,
adjusting his glasses, reading the paper.
When his needle is inserted,
I expect him to shake his head and say,
"I work all day and come home to this."

He reminds me of my friend Will,
Will who fought in three wars,
was bayoneted in the Philippines and Korea,
Will who is jobless and owes support,
who gave blood here twice a week for months
until it screwed up his gamma globulin.

Why am I here—I'm not broke like Will
or the Indian woman in the hallway
trying to keep her children quiet.
She has already given once within two days
and has hours left to wait.

I thought it would be easier than work:
just show up and do as they say,
let the receptionist assess my veins,
prick my finger for blood,
stand when the doctor checks my heart.

But there is a tiredness I didn't expect
that makes this ten dollars hard to spend,
a tiredness that won't be relieved by sleep
like after a day of unloading trucks
or by the steak dinner the doctor recommends.

A FIRST DAY

My first day with seventh graders,
I don't know any names.
Breasts are just beginning.
I can't tell the boys from the girls —
so it's an old joke —
especially the chubby ones.

Things begin moving: desks dragging,
tilting; books, pencils dropping;
the lips of a boy in front mumbling.
"Question?" I ask.
"Oh, I was just singing."
The whole room whirls with hands.

A woman enters.
The clap of her clipboard stills them.
They look down at their hands
like absent-minded owners
scolded at a pet class.
She'll be back, thank God.

Our lesson is *Johnny Tremain*,
when the Bostonians brew salt-water tea.
Too many raise their hands to read —
are they tricking me? —
even slower ones who'll be laughed at.
But they read and read and want to read.

Hasn't the word hooted across the field yet
from the gym teacher, the baseball coach
who nearly played in the majors,
as a boy leaves softball early?
When will the word hoot across the field,
taunting the mild deserter all the way
to his singing drill in the music room?

Hasn't the word come up the row yet
from the sleek night stalker
slouching asleep far in back
as he rubs his eyes to what's on?
When will the word come up the row,
sounding tough as cleats on tile,
that reading aloud isn't cool?

What if it isn't the word, but me?
—a father bringing out heavy books,
helping his children with history
until they drowse forward like drunks
or squirm free pleading,
"You always tell us more than we need!"
—a mother insisting on silverware ways,
literature nibbled with delicate forks.

For now,
the woman with the clipboard hasn't returned,
thank God, though we needed her,
as we needed moments of song,
moments of hands straying toward the ceiling,
and moments like these, just before the bell,
when everyone is following along
as a girl, her face splotched by an old burn,
reads about Johnny Tremain's crippled hand.

HALL MONITOR

A year from now I'll run into Derryl
with his Sony cassette recorder,
suitcase-size, strapped to his side,
blasting a song by Dr. Funkenstein.
I'll attempt his new handshake;
then down the store aisle he'll shout
for Dejon to grab him a Pepsi too.
Dejon, before I can feel uneasy,
will be bobbing in front of me, smiling,
mouthing lyrics into an invisible mike.

Maybe. Now, however, is now:
wrong words in a crowded hallway,
cigarettes crumpled, hard kicks,
a metal wastebasket to the head,
and Dejon is going to kill
or at least slash Derryl good.
I don't know who started it
or who did what to whom or why.
Derryl silent is stumbling back,
Dejon hissing is stalking in.

Steel blade swishing,
his back to me a split second,
I could—do grab his upper arms,
pull, my hands like ropes sliding,
tightening at the hoofs of his hands.
Tighten, talk, tighten, talk,
his knife a sharp tooth snarling,
until Derryl is far on his way
where a year from now we'll meet
in the steady beat of Dr. Funkenstein.

FOR BRENDA

I am not able to say this
eloquently –
you know,
like these lines from Rilke:

"Love consists in this, that two solitudes
protect and touch and greet each other."

An enlightened jeweler would buy that without biting
to adorn bracelets,
dangle from earrings.

I am not able to say this like that;
you would be annoyed by the jangle
of my *howevers* and *buts*.

The way I am saying this
is with words –
you know,
like what a friend sends back from Africa:

awkward constructions of tape,
cardboard,
and shredded newspaper

but addressed to you
with promises of carvings and glassware.

THE EMPTY ROOM

Karen,
in the empty room
the room of floor and walls
with hallways leading
to hallways
don't kid around
when the big ugly guy
with his ax in the air
shows up
don't go fleeing
like before
screaming down hallways
till he grabs and slobbers,
"So you want to die?
I'll take your head."

Karen,
don't kid around
sobbing
pleading
your hands in prayer
of anything, anything
as he cocks his ax
as he asks your last words
don't burst into laughter
don't slap him on the back
as if he's bought you a beer
and say,
"Kill me, kill me,
this is only a dream.
Ha-ha!"

Karen,
in the empty room
the room of floor and walls
with hallways leading
to hallways
when the big ugly guy
cocks his ax
dream or not
don't kid around.

THE MAN AT THE WHEEL

He lives in it,
a 1960 Ford convertible
on blocks in a relative's back yard.
The rumor isn't true
that at night he revs it,
spinning the tires furiously.
The engine hangs on a chain,
huge, dripping fluid
like a creature dragged
from the floor of the sea.

I don't know what else is missing.
Afternoons he sits at the wheel,
top down, reading old papers
as if he's early for an appointment.
Kids who take a shortcut
hardly notice him in the scatter
of boards, mattresses, bricks, appliances
in a yard where it's uncertain
what is being saved
or thrown away.

TWO

THROUGH MY LIFE

Upright pianos back to back
play through my life.

One seems new, its dark wood gleaming
like a groomed horse before a race.

A girl sitting with back straight
practices part of a Mozart sonata.
When she finishes,
the piano becomes furniture
beneath fine doilies and framed pictures.

The other is old and settled in a room
like a rusted car in a pasture.

A boy singing solo
senses the piano player's signals.
Relatives gathered
join the refrain of "Aura Lee"
as the boy sneaks drops of whiskey into a cup.

Upright pianos back to back
play through my life —

I am leaning between them,
listening.

PRISON CAMP NO. 3, NEAR TOKYO
For my father

Christmas Day, 1944.
His buddies wait around in light snow,
all aware of their usual hunger.
It is her first package to get through.

His bone fingers plunge and surface
through shredded newspaper,
bringing up a baseball,
then another,
then three pair of men's briefs,
then a box of homemade chocolates,
each candy kindly wrapped in cellophane.

Briefs will make warm patches.
"Your ma won't understand such extravagance," they joke.
"She thinks you're touring with Babe Ruth."
Soon no one is talking
as mouths disregard wrappers,
become wild and full.

HIGHLAND, 1955

Six in the morning, a weekday in May,
Mother is asleep, dead tired—
five children in seven years.
Dad is in the kitchen rehearsing his music.

Back from Bataan, back to work,
he sells insurance day and night.
Saturdays in spring he sings weddings
for extra money we always need.

His baritone voice
someday Dennis, my brother, will imitate so well
that company in another room will become quiet,
saying, "Sh, Bernie's singing."

But that is another story years away.
This is six in the morning, a weekday in May,
the kitchen windows wide open
and Mrs. Krause next door listening.

Later she will confide to Mother,
"I wish Art would sing to me in the morning
like Bernie does to you."

SATURDAY NIGHT

A butterfly
Mother in yellow dress
free of pedal pushers
faded blouse

perfume
we are drawn
to her dark brown curls
her face calm
beautiful
like Bernadette at Lourdes
picture hidden
with my baseball cards

leaving
Dad turns the back light on
to guard us
guide them both home safe
and we promise her
this time really will
do what the sitter says
and not fight ever again

BICYCLE SPRING

Windy, sunny, and Sunday,
the afternoon of your father's promise,
you will learn to ride your bike:

your father breathing hard
pushes, runs at your side,
one hand on the handlebars,
the other firm on the seat,

launching you like a glider
to soar long seconds
before wobbling to crash
in the soft green field

until you know how to ride
suddenly except for the brakes
and your father suddenly
is a speck waving way behind

as you pedal toward strange sights
in blocks where he
has forbidden you to walk.

THE LINE HOME

One afternoon in kindergarten,
standing second in the line home
behind Bobby Leonard,
the best boy in our class,
I jabbed for no reason
a stiff needle from the Christmas tree
into his quiet face.

It felt good, but after his long scream
Miss Ronan sentenced me to the very end,
though it was my first crime
and I could tie my shoes
and tell time.

There when we left school
and finally crossed the busy street,
the bad kids yelled and shoved
but were never fastest home

like Bobby Leonard,
whose mother we never saw
until a morning in second grade
when she burst in searching
our book bags and coats
for Robert's missing boot.

SNEAKING IN THE STATE FAIR

As the fat sheriff who's taken
a week's vacation from his job as a clerk
and who shakes his billy like a threatening scepter
turns his horse and trots far the other way,
boys swarm into the cyclone fence
like flies flat into a screen toward light,
then scramble upward to the scarring top
where their wild fingers become careful and pluck
wires harsh with rusted barbs
as the sheriff rears and as hoofs throb closer,
they grunt working up their dangling legs
clumsy, straining like bags of sand
as his club nears, whacking the fence,
demanding the meek admission fee,
boys squatting at last on the swaying wires
bounce like frightened divers about to leap
from a distant board into a speck of a pool,
then in a launching cheer they leap—
land hard scraping palms and knees,
the last sprawled as if he'd never get up,
but with that red shout of "Stop those kids!"
they all pass a popcorn man on break,
who goes along with the whacking and shouting
by yanking off his special cap and lurching
forward from his chair and his nap to
                                    wink
as they slip into thin spaces in the crowd
that bumps slowly over sawdust toward the rides.

WHIPPING

"You two quit or else!"
But we were tall like him,
no longer dreaded his threats,
so we kept making noise:

we were The Crusher and Mr. M.
It was elbow stabs and stomach claws,
airplane spins and body slams,
until he started up the stairs.

Muffling our laughs
as his belt stung
as he yelled, "You sons of bitches!"
we faked, like our favorite wrestlers,
groans of incredible pain,

but after,
when we heard him in his room
breathing like a man who'd been chased,
we were ashamed—
it was our last whipping.

CHARACTERS

Aunt Duly is here wallpapering our kitchen.
She is seventy-one years old
but still paints silos and moves pianos.
If I bet her, she will touch her palms
to the floor without bending her knees.

When she first sees me, long hair and beard,
she comes down the ladder waving her brush:
"Judas Priest, Kev, when I was a girl,
they used to beat guys like you with chairs."

She has been going up and down this last hour
as if her ladder is an escalator,
telling me about drunken gravediggers
or the grocer who wouldn't serve lawyers.
I'm afraid she'll slip or faint,

but she is coming down the ladder,
telling me about Barney Ruckle in the back pew
quietly mocking each bead during the rosary:
"Gimme a nickel, Mary. Gimme a nickel, Mary.
Gimme a nickel . . ."

Going up the ladder
because she really does have work to do,
she pauses halfway and says,
"You know, they're all dead now,
all those characters who used to make us laugh."

SCHOONER BAR

Thoughts of you
red coals from a forgotten dream
Tonight I saw my breath
ghost stalking early September
If you were here
returning through years
to the round table in back
we could drink hot rums until closing
as large wet flakes
turn the dark streets white
Our footsteps through snow would be new
Our love necessary
like shelter
like heat

THREE

REPEAT AFTER ME

The Doberman pinscher
properly trained
has a sane mind.

WHATEVER HAPPENED

How persuasive our corporations—
I've willingly paid them,

Chrysler across my baseball cap,
McDonald's golden arches
spanning my sweatshirt,
my red gym bag labeled
like a two-gallon can of Coke,

and today I passed a woman
with a Camel Lights tattoo.

God bless America.

TWO CITIES

It's still there,
paint chipped and signless,
the pole which once proclaimed
in the middle of the Lake Street bridge
MINNEAPOLIS   ST. PAUL
whose side you were on —
essential one spring
when these cities seethed an hour apart
over daylight savings.

I'd forgotten that, until this morning
at dawn driving from Minneapolis:
those streetlights, west of the pole, were already off,
while those east, St. Paul, blazed orange.
I shifted up Marshall hill
checking my rearview mirror.

So they're still at it . . .
as if O'Brien's Bar, gone years,
were open again serving St. Paul,
where Harry tells off a customer
who admits being from Minneapolis,
"Get the hell out,
you're all Swedes or Republicans!"
which rattles my friend Jim,
a colonel's son who has lived all over
and has cornered me with his hope
of one world in this lifetime.

THAT LEAVES YOU AND ME

John has six eggs.
He can only carry five home comfortably.
How many must John throw at the bus?
The answer is obvious as a rubber raft
sinking slowly in heavy seas
with one adult too many aboard.

You know who's *not* going over:
a scientist who may change the world,
a mother nursing her child,
a soldier bayoneted in three wars,
and, of course, a priest.

This leaves John juggling in his right hand
a sixty-year-old man who has lived his life
and a convicted murderer sentenced to die.
Each gives an excellent excuse.
Who now?
Shall we take their places?

I'm the one,
a thirty-year-old man on unemployment again.
I don't want to die —
I know I'll go over disgustingly,
thrown like egg on a bus window.
And you?
Next time you consider this problem,
how will you go over?

STANDARD OPERATIONS
"Icarus, my son, I charge you to keep a middle course."

Icarus frantic in his wax-dripping wings,
feathers fluttering loose
from soaring too near the sun,
collapses upon the placid sea.

His father continues his moderate flight.
"He didn't keep within himself,"
the sports announcer cautions
as if we're more than football fans

but disciples of a TV mystic
who describes a halfback bursting
through a hole so fleetly
he leaves behind the invaluable ball.

And once again I am a skittish senior
the Army recruiter must soothe toward signature.
"Your friend would have his leg today
if he'd followed open-field procedures."

SIGNS

A company park always watched:
THIS AREA UNDER CAMERA SURVEILLANCE
I am afraid tonight, walking,
and think of a yellow sign,
black letters thick as shotgun shells,
posted on our school one spring:
NO HARDBALL PLAYING
We didn't, either, until June,
then all summer watched,
fearing the principal would appear,
a game warden pouncing on poachers,
confiscating until fall our bats and gloves.

Today the park was a corral:
men and women picketing
the production of nuclear bombs
were prodded here and surrounded
long enough to film faces.
The rational method
perfected during Vietnam —
no tear gas or bashed heads;
the leaders then a few days later
in the dark calm before dawn
would be taken from their homes.

VITA-CISE
An exercise program throughout the park
landscaped with red markers
like golf
or Stations of the Cross,
a scientifically proven pilgrimage
granting those seeking long life
cardiovascular benefits.
"Do 10 burpies. Advance"
over the winding running path.

FOR THE ENJOYMENT OF
EMPLOYEES AND COMMUNITY
What's left,
that is,
of community,
a few crumbling houses
crowded by parking ramps.

I live in a duplex here.
The kids were chased from the park long ago
for playing made-up games,
tackle football on their knees,

and the old woman who picks the street
of aluminum cans and returnable bottles,
her tiny white dog sniffing ahead
as she pulls her wealth in a shopping cart,
never comes this far:
ALCOHOL PROHIBITED

She knows this is no respectable park
for scruffy characters brash with wine.
They'd jab green bottles skyward,
seeing the surveillance sign,
and chant an impromptu commercial,
"What's the word? Thunderbird!
What's the price? Fifty twice!"

All through every night
for the safety of late workers,
floodlights blaze
from the top tiers of parking ramps,
grilling houses below
like ringleaders of a movement
the powerful are determined to break.

I have a college degree and a job.
I thought I could just leave
when the light finally got to me,
and the others who couldn't
or who would stay anyway
could still get by,
the blues piano player next door
performing at bars,
passing an empty pitcher through the crowd.

NUCLEAR MISSILES AREN'T EVIL
IT'S HOW THEY'RE USED
An executive explained to a demonstrator.
I look across the deserted park,
signs of this thinking,
blocks leveled flat for an exercise course,
the enjoyment of employees and community
under camera surveillance,
and along the curbs,
as if a way of life has vanished,
remains of old driveways.

LAID OFF

For years
he had a jingle of keys,
a fine stringer.

Quitting time
he is like a man suddenly losing
tufts of hair all over his body.

His key chain holds on
to house key
and car

key,
which feels suspiciously
as if a second bomb
is wired to the ignition.

PIONEER CEMETERY

I hurry into the woods,
slapping bugs and branches aside,
almost twisting an ankle
when the path turns a clay slush.

You slow. "Black-eyed Susans!"
The graveyard's a half-hour hike.
"They add so much to bouquets."
I've a noon meeting in Duluth.

Green darkness opens to a sunlit hill:
Pioneer Resting Place,
stone fragments fallen all over,
scythed grass the only sign of remembrance.

44 YEARS, 3 MONTHS, 4 DAYS
Is this a grave or part of one?
You pull chunks from thick brush:
REPUBLIC   LOVING   HUSBAND OF

How we honor them . . .
Were these like your great-grandfather
who blasted rock to build our streets,
who dug our sewer ditches?

Going back, we take our time.
Surprised by raspberries ripe this early,
we pick our hats full and eat.
My meeting can wait.

I'll have a granite gravestone, please,
weatherproofed, too heavy to heave
and too hard even for some drunk's boot.
"You're not funny."

I'm not. Those ruins remind me
of white seconds between sleep and waking
when I don't know if the light
is dawn or dusk or what.

CASH FOR GUNS

How matter-of-fact my sister seems
as she describes some jerk
who on all fours and barking
leaped at her from a factory door,
his pals hidden inside hooting . . .

A lifelong American —
it's a legal right, isn't it,
to walk a sidewalk unharassed?

Last week at CASH FOR GUNS
when I stopped to look at tents,
a man at the pistol counter,
speaking quietly to the clerk,
wanted something light
his wife could shoot.

She stood outside the discussion.
Her eyes staring at a far wall
scare me now,
like this look in my sister's eyes —
recruits raw and ready for arms.

SHOPLIFTER: 7-ELEVEN

When his crutches slip
on wet winter floor
the frozen pizzas under his coat
wobble off like tires toward
a manager trainee who
as if it's in some manual
grabs up the crutches

he rests where he is
on floor waiting for police
asks for coffee
as the trainee dreams
that he crawls for the door
like a seal through slush

ALLIGATOR ISLAND
An island somewhere in the third world

Watch your step:
the gators are extinct,
but tacks ooze a toothy tetanus.
Toxic waste from America:

officials split the dumping fees,
the poor receive platitudes —
"Every person can enjoy
a fresh breeze and bright moon."

A bought-out hospital
topped by a landing tower
blots the sky.
Helicopters around the clock

pack human body parts,
harvested a few dollars each
as if this darkened island
were a foreclosed farm.

Look: a copter carrying
a load of kidneys
ascends where heaven is taught to be,
before descending blest

to that fortunate land
of fresh breezes,
bright moons,
long lives.

FOUR

MITTENS

When winter shivers me
like a swimmer dipping
into an icy pool
and though I'm wearing gloves
each finger stiffens
like a body in a long drawer,
I switch to mittens,
sheltering my fingers
like snowed-in friends
who thaw,
accept their close lodging,
and now and then
perform short skits
until the weather warms.

MODERATE LIFE

Picking this jagged glass
completely from a stranger's sidewalk
will not be remembered
for testimony on my behalf
some long sleepless night
when my memory is a bitter chatter
of bleak acts I can't deny.

I should jot it on a card,
wallet-size for emergencies,
a spare tire in finger's reach:
"Saved bare feet from laceration"—
good deeds like gold stars
until my card overflowing
could be preserved by lamination.

What if I go too far
pursuing a daily quota of deeds—
would I harass old people with help,
then after years of laminating cards
pin them like armor plates
over my softest spots
and rage nasty as a crazed armadillo?

I attempt a moderate life:
no liquor until it's truly dark,
a cigarette or two at most each day,
then throw away the pack.
Arrangements can be made:
each completed card perhaps
in the custody of a careful friend.

A BOX OF POPCORN

Why be shy?
Why stay at home?
Unless your appearance
is disturbing—
let's say you wear a German helmet
touring a veterans' home—
a box of popcorn
is all you need.

A giant box is best.
You have all afternoon.
White cardboard
with blue-red rockets flaring
is standard,
recognized at once
as a box of popcorn,
casual as a Frisbee
or plaid Bermudas.

Let's take the park:
munch naturally—
you have all afternoon—
lean back on a bench,
explore the paved trail
or stray through sumac and long grass,
and if perhaps you stumble on lovers,
their bodies gleaming through green brush,
smile,
but if they should protest, as if you
sat on them in a dark theater,
offer them popcorn.
Save some for the ducks.

FAVORITE RECIPE

Flapping on my windshield
what appears to be a parking ticket
or complaint about my wild lawn
is a recipe,
anonymous,
for German chocolate caramel bars.

This can't be for me:
I ruin ready-serve soup.
Still, I follow the green ink swirling
into a first line opening
like a sensual memo:
"Melt 50 caramels in a double boiler."

I read on, sensing blue heat
softening the caramel cubes,
shredded coconut,
chocolate chips,
until I am mixing in milk
warm from milking,
butter from the movie theater,
handfuls of chopped walnuts
when a sprinkle is called for.

A favorite recipe,
a special perhaps at potluck dinners,
I could cherish it,
let it become brittle in a book
like a leaf or lock of hair,
but it ends with
"Pass It On,"
as if someone is dying.
I am the closest relative.

HANDICAPPED

Impatiently,
like a jogger stopped by traffic,
I wait on the sidewalk:
men and women in wheelchairs
motor from the art gallery,
one after one after one
received and loaded
on the power lift of their special van.
A thought mutters:
these people couldn't survive
without high technology.
As if I could
continue as I am,
getting through to my car,
which will cross the Mississippi in seconds
over a bridge necessary as any prosthesis,
in minutes reach downtown St. Paul,
where up twelve floors by elevator
I arrive dry
and not unusually late.

BODY WORK

I sit in an office,
a clean air-conditioned place,
making phone calls, signing forms,
an easy job physically,
but after work my body's slow,
blood sluggish like cooled oil.

Exercise won't help.
My body in shape for a triathlon
could never crank water
from the iron pump in my yard,
ornamental as the pink flamingo
poised near the dry spout.

I want, for a half-hour or so,
to sweat like a construction worker
steadying high on a scaffold
a wheelbarrow of bricks
as he makes something important,
a parking lot into a school.

Imagine this:
thousands of us after work
cracking a comparable sweat
as we jog on treadmills
together at the Civic Center,
spinning giant generators.

What revolutions we'd make!
A city's worth of light and heat
from morning pastries and pasta lunches.
Think of the jobs alone
in forbidden foods.
Great balls of fire!

OEDIPUS UPDATE
In the voice of Laius, father of Oedipus

We live together
but never talk of marriage.
I practice piano after work,
long to play in a jazz band.
She runs a frame shop, even weekends,
and evenings studies French.

Our son isn't conceived yet,
so he's not abandoned,
crying clamped and soiled
at the base of some brambled hill
until he grows unwittingly able
to kill me and marry his mother.

She won't be a suicide.
He's going to murder her
in this version, when he learns
at the ends of these aspiring days
what little's left for affection.

Still, we don't think of him uneasily,
like an eight-pound hot potato,
but in perspective, like a bank notice
for a balloon payment due
eventually but not this year.

PENNY MAN

The bank teller frowns at him.
"Where did you get those?" she asks,
as if he'd smashed a gumball machine.
A quart jar full of pennies —

and the coin counter doesn't work.
He'll have to count them
one by one into dollars,
a long test in front of her.

I'm wondering too how he does it.
He never works steady —
still, always pennies
for milk, bread,
even cigarettes and beer.

As I wait in line,
two men behind me worry
about a shutdown at work;
a woman near the front curses,
her pension check smaller.

I don't know about them,
or you,
wherever you are in line,
whether the penny man's a bother,
like someone who speaks little English
buying stamps slowly at the post office,

but I'm listening to him
shaking out that jar and counting
coin after coin:
an Oriental master
showing tricks
on the abacus.

ANNIVERSARY

Asking an afternoon off,
I leave alone to celebrate
five years of working here,
knowing well my cleared desk
will soon be crammed with files.
Sweet white wine,
T-shirt and my tattered jeans –
I joke and sing in the park,
but when I refuse them spare change,
the drunken men move away.
None of them remembers me –
five years since I worked day labor.

All the detailed regulations and forms –
more and more I'm becoming
as compulsive as the gas-station attendant
on downtown Robert Street
who bursts into brief rages
when stopped to decipher directions
or answer an insistent phone.
"I've got my work," he roars,
then rushes back mop in hand
as if disaster clamors
to scrub the concrete even cleaner.

Another swig – the wine swirls deeper.
I see Lorraine, our overburdened clerk,
chain-smoking into collapse,
staring back from her stretcher
at her desk loaded with work.
She whimpers she's way behind,
doesn't have time to go,
nor die that very night,
nine hundred sick-leave hours
never used.

I chug what wine is left
as the park darkens with evening.
Down the street the poor gather
for dinner at Dorothy Day.
Impatiently a woman paces in front
as she does always all over downtown,
a bald spot bright in the back of her head.
She is calling my name as always,
calling her missing child home.

I can't go to her,
nor to any of them,
the drunken men,
the anxious attendant,
Lorraine,
though I hear them all.
Tomorrow at work
I'll show up sobered.

STARS, WATER, WIND, TIME
For Tina

I hardly remember
those months of winter
before I met you—
mornings pacing the neighborhood,
the sidewalk a long hallway.

Tonight
all the traffic lights are green
going my way
driving to you.
I am snow reflecting
these city stars,

snow melting,
running along curbs
toward the Mississippi.
And if some prankster's dam
backs the street up
or, more likely,
my bald tire
blows flat,

I'll get out
and walk
under real stars,
this warm March wind,
which tonight could topple
fields of eroded monuments,
gusting behind,
going my way
closer to you.

Kevin FitzPatrick was born in 1949 in St. Paul, Minnesota, and was educated at the University of Minnesota and the College of St. Thomas. He has edited the *Lake Street Review* since 1977. Besides coordinating the Lake Street Writers' Workshop and teaching poetry and fiction writing, he has been a postal clerk, ice-cube factory worker, park grounds keeper, bartender, crime researcher, self-defense instructor, job developer, sports director, and claims examiner.